THE NIGHT SKY

and Other
Amazing Sights
in Space

Nick Hunter

Raintree is an imprint of Capstone Global Library Limited, a company incorporated in England and Wales having its registered office at 7 Pilgrim Street, London, EC4V 6LB – Registered company number: 6695582

www.raintreepublishers.co.uk
myorders@raintreepublishers.co.uk

Text © Capstone Global Library Limited 2013
First published in hardback in 2013
First published in paperback in 2014
The moral rights of the proprietor have been asserted.

Edited by Dan Nunn, Rebecca Rissman, and Sian Smith
Designed by Joanna Hinton-Malivoire and Marcus Bell
Picture research by Mica Brancic
Production by Sophia Argyris
Originated by Capstone Global Library Ltd
Printed and bound in China

ISBN 978 1 406 25959 9 (hardback)
17 16 15 14 13
10 9 8 7 6 5 4 3 2 1

ISBN 978 1 406 25960 5 (paperback)
18 17 16 15 14
10 9 8 7 6 5 4 3 2 1

British Library Cataloguing in Publication Data
Hunter, Nick.
The night sky and other amazing sights in space.
  1. Astronomy--Juvenile literature.
  I. Title
  520-dc23

Acknowledgements
We would like to thank the following for permission to reproduce photographs: Alamy pp.12 (© Images of Africa Photobank/David Keith Jones), 33 (© Mark Hamilton); Capstone Publishers pp.44, 45 (© Karon Dubke); Getty Images pp4 (Photolibrary/Steven Puetzer), 10 (AFP Photo), 11 (AFP Photo/Damien Meyer); NASA pp.19, 15 (JPL-Caltech/R. Hurt (SSC)), 21 (Solar & Heliospheric Observatory), 22 (SOHO), 26 (University of Maryland/JPL-Caltech), 30 (JPL-Caltech/UCLA), 37 (ESA, M. Robberto (Space Telescope Science Institute/ESA) and the Hubble Space Telescope Orion Treasury Project Team), 38 (ESA/SOHO), 40 (SDO), 41 (Visible Earth/EOS Project Science Office/Goddard Space Flight Centre), 42 (JAXA), 43 (ESA/Johns Hopkins University); Science Photo Library pp.8 (Gary Hincks), 13, 14, 34 (Babak Tafreshi, Twan), 23 (NASA), 24 (Walter Pacholka, Astropics), 25 (Richard Kail), 27 (European Southern Observatory), 28 (Detlev Van Ravenswaay), 29 (Julian Baum), 31 (Alex Cherney, Terrastro.com), 32 (Jerry Lodriguss), 35 (Roger Harris), 39 (Julian Baum); Shutterstock pp.5 (© Albie Bredenhann), 6 (© Kokhanchikov), 7 (© sdecoret), 9 (© Viktar Malyshchyts), 17 (© Roman Krochuk), 17 (© Stephen Mcsweeny), 18 (© Leonello Calvetti), 20 (© Triff); WIYN and NOAO/AURA/NSF//University of Alaska Anchorage/T. A. Rector p36.

Cover photograph of Comet McNaught reproduced with permission of Miroslav Druckmüller.

We would like to thank Stuart Atkinson for his invaluable help in the preparation of this book.

Contents

Some words are shown in bold, **like this**. You can find them in the glossary on page 46.

Earth in space

Look up into the sky and you can see some amazing sights. On a clear night you will see hundreds of lights. These are the **stars** and **planets**. They share the **universe** with our own planet, Earth.

You can look for stars and planets in the night sky. Stars twinkle, but planets do not.

4

The Moon is the closest natural object to Earth in space.

The brightest light in the night sky is usually the Moon. It is smaller than stars and planets in space, but it looks large to us because it is much closer to Earth.

By day, we don't usually see the Moon. During the day, the brightest light in the sky is the Sun. The Sun is our nearest **star**. It gives us light and warmth.

Daylight comes from the Sun, even when the sky is cloudy.

From space, you can see where it is daytime and nighttime on Earth.

Earth spins around every 24 hours. In daytime, we are facing the Sun. The other side of the world is facing away from the Sun. It is nighttime there.

Earth moves around the Sun in a path called an **orbit**. Earth takes a year to travel all the way around the Sun. The Moon travels around the Earth in the same way. It takes about 27 days for the Moon to move around Earth.

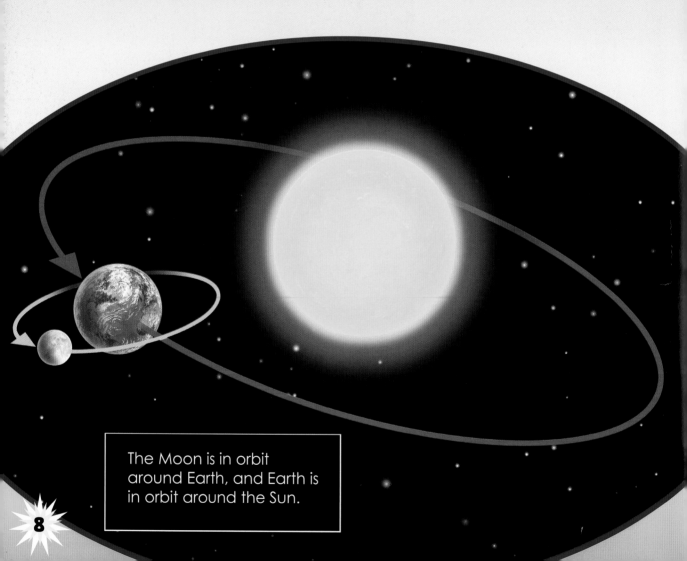

The Moon is in orbit around Earth, and Earth is in orbit around the Sun.

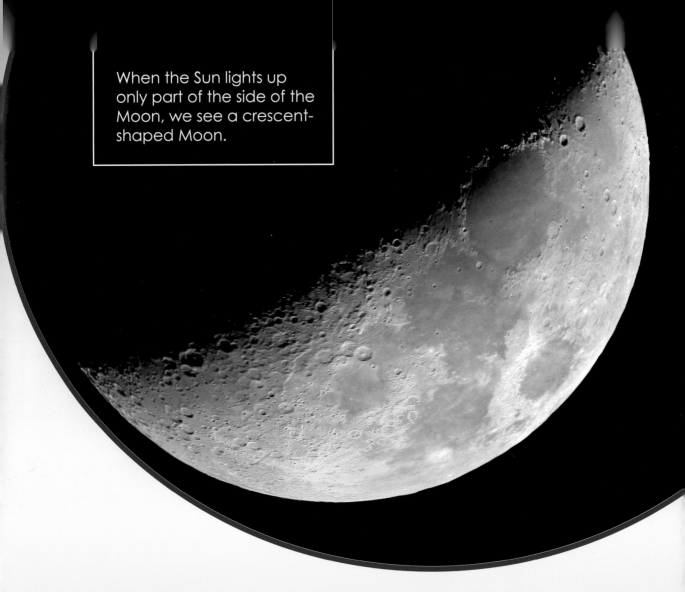

When the Sun lights up only part of the side of the Moon, we see a crescent-shaped Moon.

The Moon does not make light itself. We see the Moon because light from the Sun shines on it. As the Moon and Earth change position, we see different parts of the Moon light up.

9

Solar eclipses

Sometimes you can see an amazing sight in the daytime. When the Moon passes between Earth and the Sun, it blocks out some or all of the Sun. This is called a solar eclipse.

These people are wearing special glasses to protect their eyes from the Sun's rays while watching an eclipse.

WARNING!

You should never look directly at the Sun. This can damage your eyes.

Slowly, the dark disc of the Moon blocks out the Sun.

At first, the Moon starts to cross the Sun. It looks as if someone has taken a bite out of the Sun. The bite slowly gets bigger.

At last, the Sun is completely covered by the Moon. The sky goes dark. This is a **total eclipse of the Sun**. The Sun's outer layer appears as a bright circle around the Moon.

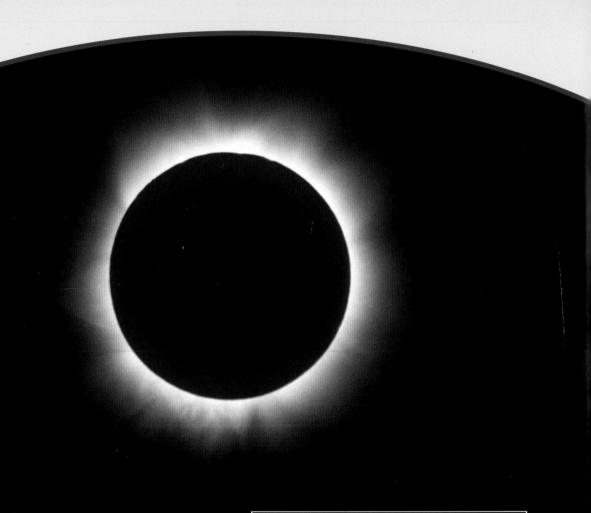

This total eclipse was seen from Kenya in Africa.

The Sun can be totally covered for several minutes, or just a few seconds.

Slowly, the Moon begins to move, uncovering the surface of the Sun once more. The first rays of light shine through. It looks like the sparkle of a diamond ring in the sky.

Solar eclipses happen because the Moon passes between the Sun and Earth. How can the Moon block out the Sun when it is much smaller than the Sun?

These pictures show the stages of a solar eclipse over the Pacific Ocean.

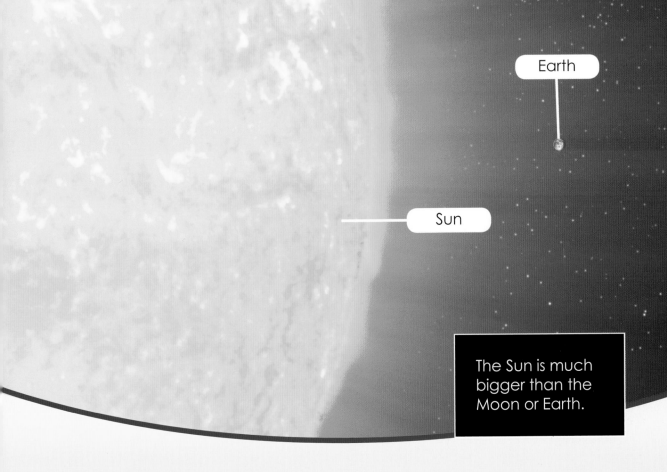

Earth

Sun

The Sun is much bigger than the Moon or Earth.

Although the Sun is around 400 times bigger than the Moon, the Moon is 400 times closer to Earth. This means that they look the same size in the sky.

The Northern Lights

There are many other incredible sights in the night sky. The Northern Lights are one of the most exciting light shows you could ever see. They can start with a pale green light in the sky.

Amazing lights like this only appear on some nights.

These campers have travelled to see the Northern Lights.

Sometimes, they become beautiful, bright sheets of light dancing across the night sky. The Northern Lights are called an **aurora**. Their full name is the aurora borealis.

The Northern Lights are most often seen in places close to the North Pole. Sometimes people in northern Europe and even Scotland can see the Northern Lights, too.

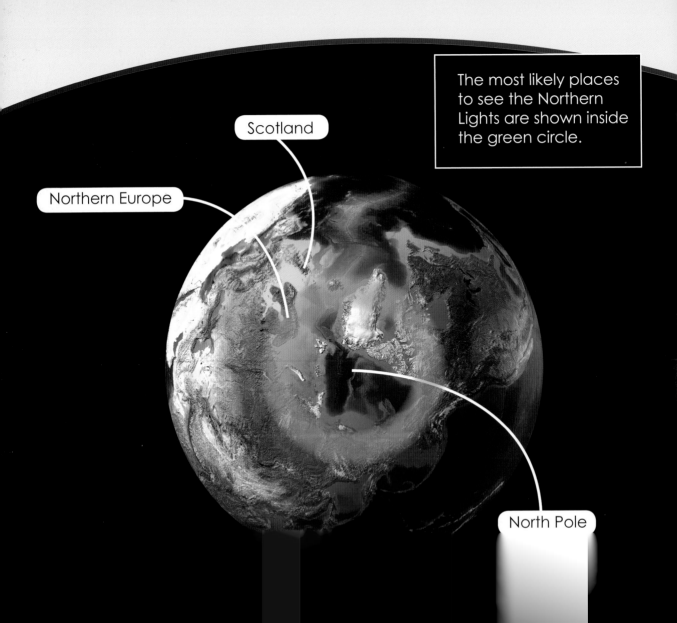

The most likely places to see the Northern Lights are shown inside the green circle.

Scotland

Northern Europe

North Pole

Astronauts can also see the Northern Lights from space!

The Northern Lights form high above the ground. They are usually around 100 kilometres up in Earth's **atmosphere**.

19

The Northern Lights are caused by the Sun. The Sun sends out a **solar wind**, as well as light and heat. The solar wind is an invisible stream of tiny **particles** of **energy**. These particles move across the **solar system** like a wind.

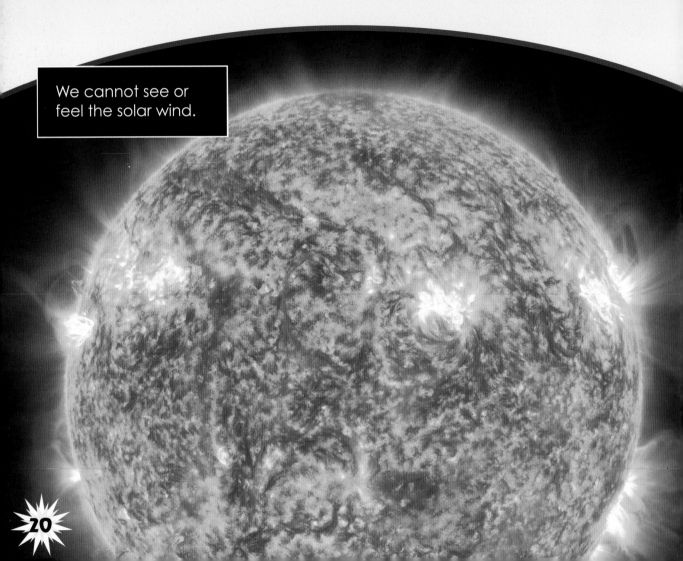

We cannot see or feel the solar wind.

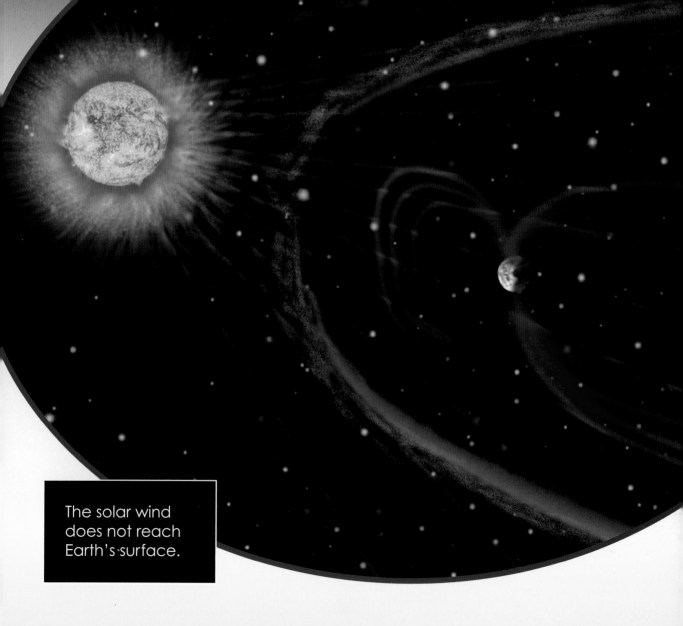

The solar wind does not reach Earth's surface.

We can see the effects of the solar wind when it causes the Northern Lights. The light show is made by the solar wind hitting Earth's **atmosphere**.

Earth is like a giant magnet with a **magnetic field** around it. Earth's magnetic field pushes the **particles** of the **solar wind** away from the **planet**.

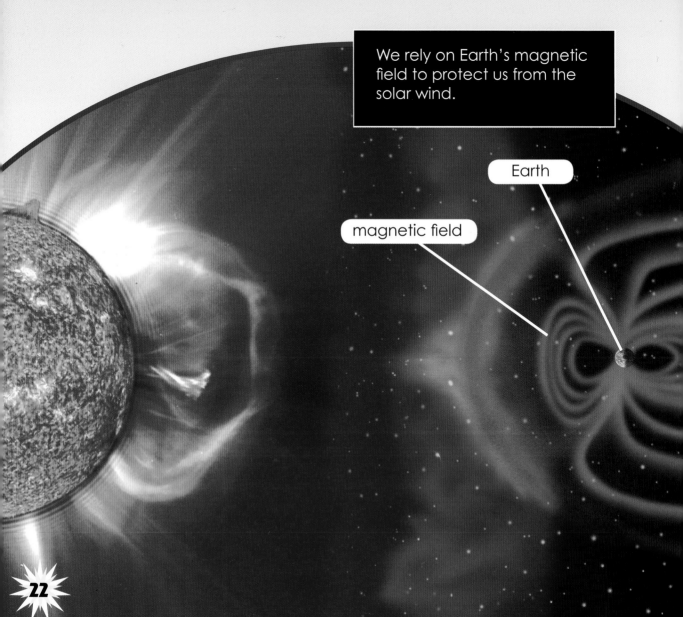

We rely on Earth's magnetic field to protect us from the solar wind.

Earth

magnetic field

This picture shows the South Pole, with the Southern Lights dancing around it.

The particles of the solar wind collect around the North and South Poles. That is why the Northern Lights can be seen near the North Pole. The South Pole has its own **aurora** called the Southern Lights.

Comets

Every so often, comets can be seen blazing through the night sky. Comets are actually large lumps of rock, dust, and ice, like huge, dirty snowballs. They are usually a few kilometres wide.

Comet Hale-Bopp appeared over California in 1997.

the Sun

comet

Comets are only close to the Sun for part of their journey.

Comets travel around the Sun. The Sun is the centre of our **solar system**. Comets can be seen from Earth when they are close to the Sun.

The comets we see from Earth were formed billions of years ago. Pieces of rock and ice clumped together to form the comet's **nucleus**. Comets may have a small **core** of solid rock.

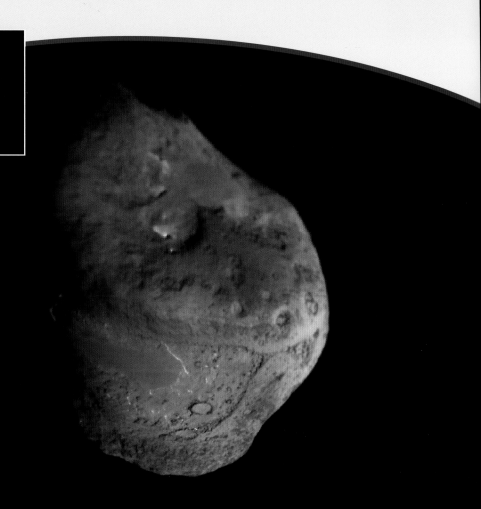

The nucleus in the middle of a comet can be many different shapes.

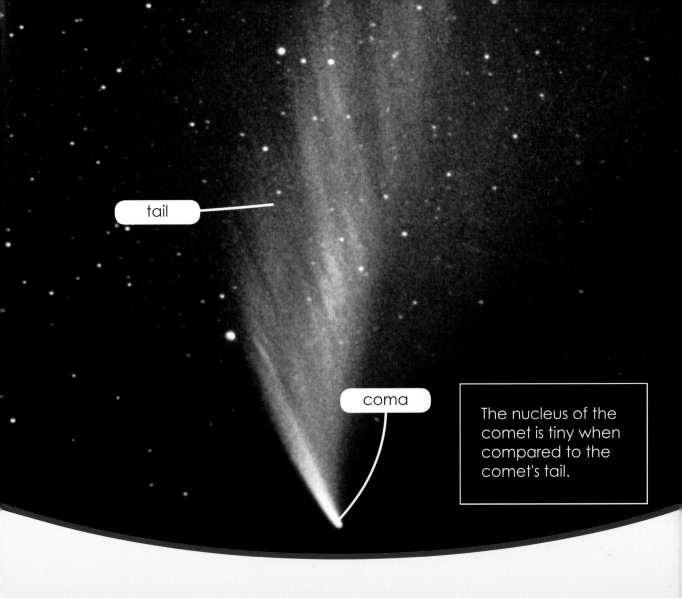

tail

coma

The nucleus of the comet is tiny when compared to the comet's tail.

When a comet gets close to the Sun, bits of ice and dust break off. They form a hazy cloud called a **coma**. A tail of ice and dust streams out behind the comet.

Comets travel billions of kilometres across the **solar system**. Some comets travel from an area called the Kuiper Belt. It is on the edge of the solar system.

Some lumps of ice and rock in the Kuiper Belt are nearly as big as **planets**.

Some comets may
have passed Earth
only once since
the time of the
dinosaurs.

Other comets come from even further
away. They come from a distant area
of space called the Oort Cloud. These
comets may take millions of years to
travel around the Sun.

The comets we see in the night sky are moving very fast. A force called **gravity** makes them move around the Sun.

The comet, Siding Spring, passed by Earth in 2009.

Comet Lovejoy flew close to the Sun in 2011.

By the time comets can be seen from Earth, their tails can be millions of miles long. Sometimes comets can even crash into the Sun.

Halley's Comet is one of the most famous comets. It can be seen from Earth every 75 years. It will next pass us in 2061. Other comets will pass Earth before then. You can look on the Internet to find out when comets are due to appear.

Halley's Comet is named after the **astronomer** Edmond Halley.

You might even be able to discover your own comet. More than 800 comets have been discovered, but new comets are found every year. One day there could be a comet named after you!

It is best to hunt for comets on a moonless night, when the sky is clear and dark.

Stars

The **stars** that light the sky above us are huge balls of burning gases. They are incredibly hot. Anything that comes too close to a star will be destroyed immediately.

Sirius

Sirius is the brightest star in the night sky.

White stars are hotter than yellow or red stars.

Not all stars are the same. Stars in the sky can glow red, yellow, or white. Stars can also be very different in size.

Stars form in giant clouds of gas and dust called **nebulas**. Over millions of years, the force of **gravity** pulls the tiny **particles** of the cloud together.

Light from the Rosette Nebula takes about 5,000 years to reach Earth.

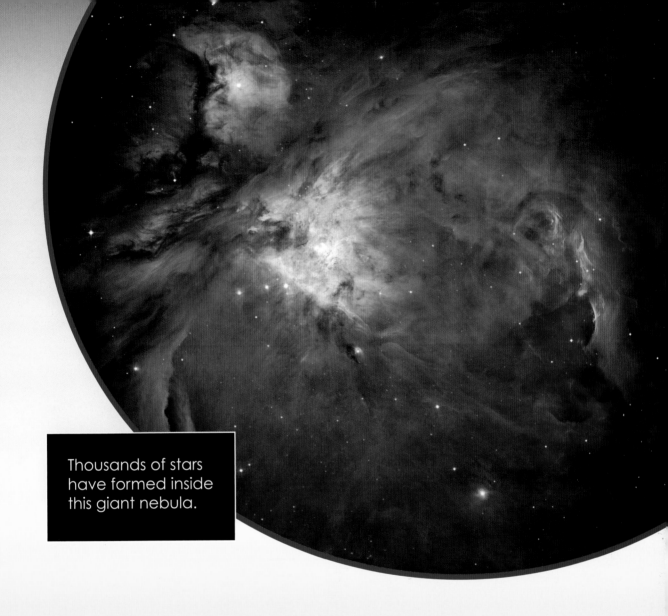

Thousands of stars have formed inside this giant nebula.

The gas and dust heat up as they come together. The cloud becomes so big and hot that **reactions** start up deep inside. They release heat and light. A new star is born.

Stars are far too hot for any person or spacecraft to visit. Scientists have launched spacecraft that **orbit** around the Sun. They collect information about how the star is changing.

This spacecraft is being used to study the Sun.

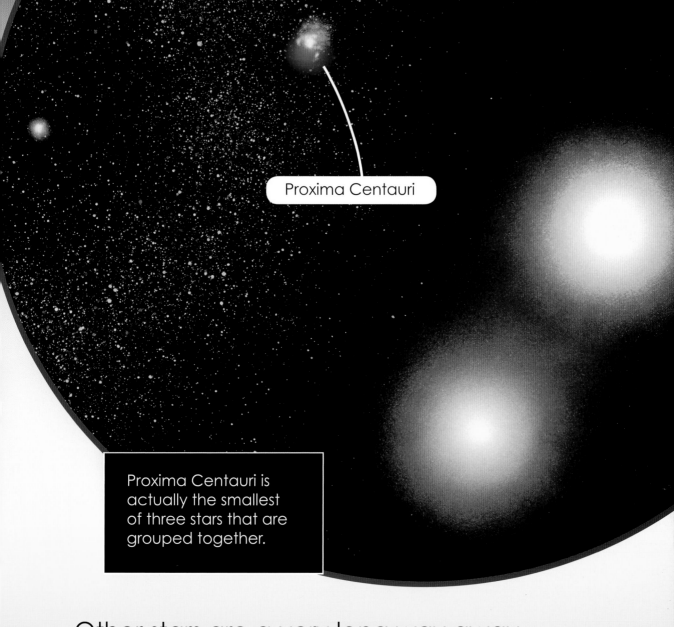

Proxima Centauri

Proxima Centauri is actually the smallest of three stars that are grouped together.

Other stars are a very long way away. After the Sun, the next closest star to Earth is Proxima Centauri. It takes four years for the light from this star to reach us.

Have you ever wondered why **stars** shine? Stars are mostly made of a material called **hydrogen**. Stars make heat and light from **reactions** going on deep inside them. The heat and light created by the reactions move through space to Earth and other **planets**.

The surface of a star is cooler than the middle, where the reactions happen.

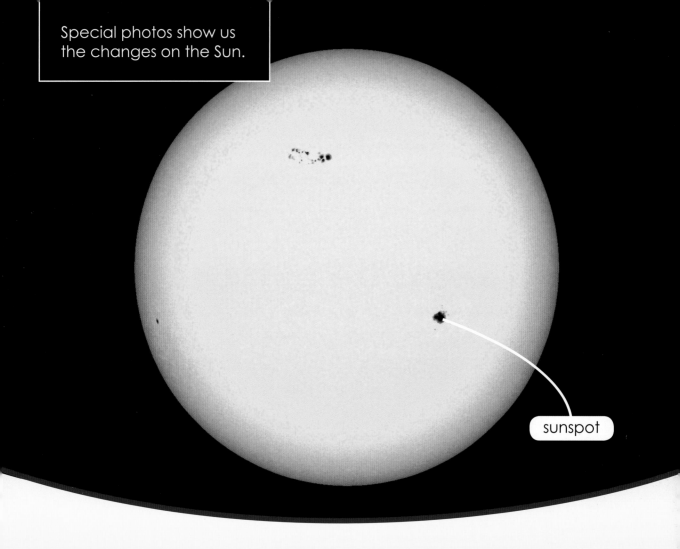

Special photos show us the changes on the Sun.

sunspot

The surface of a star is always changing and our Sun changes too. **Sunspots** are cooler areas on the Sun's surface. Sunspots on the Sun's surface seem small, but they can actually be thousands of kilometres wide.

Stars do not last forever. They change over billions of years. The Sun is an ordinary yellow star. A very long time from now, the Sun will become a huge red giant star. It will then shrink again as its fuel finally runs out.

This picture shows what the Sun could look like when it becomes a red giant star.

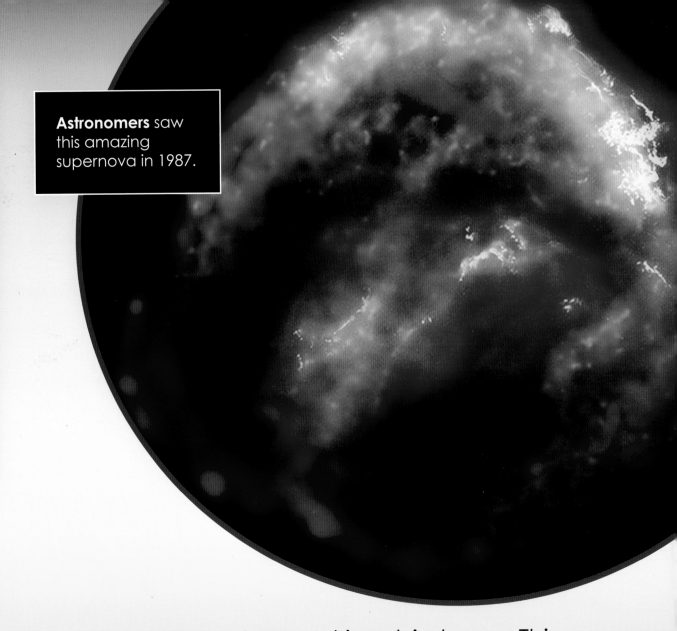

The biggest stars end in a big bang. This is called a **supernova**. The **reactions** in the star happen so fast that the whole star explodes.

43

Activity: measuring space

You will need:
- a ball
- a measuring wheel
- some friends to help measure distances
- lots of space.

Ask one friend to stand in the middle of a field, holding the ball.

If the ball is the Sun:

- Someone standing two metres from the ball would be the Earth.
- The furthest **planet** from the Sun is Neptune. It would be 60 metres away from the ball.
- The Kuiper Belt where some comets come from would be around 100 metres away.
- The nearest part of the Oort Cloud would be about 10 kilometres away!

Glossary

astronomer person who studies space and the night sky

atmosphere layer of gases that surrounds a planet such as Earth

aurora lights in the sky caused by the solar wind, such as the Northern Lights

coma cloud of gas and dust around the nucleus of a comet

core middle of an object

energy power. Heat and light are forms of energy.

gravity force that pulls all objects together

hydrogen substance from which the Sun is made and which reacts to release energy

magnetic field area where a magnet's force can be felt

nebula cloud of gas and dust from which stars and planets form

nucleus big lump of ice and rock at the centre of a comet

orbit path that an object in space takes as it moves around another object, such as when Earth goes around the Sun; also the act of moving along that path

particle tiniest possible piece of a material

planet large object (usually made of rock or gas) that orbits a star. Our planet Earth orbits the Sun.

reaction when chemicals or materials change

solar system the Sun and the eight planets and other small objects that travel around it

solar wind stream of particles that flows from the Sun

star huge ball of burning gas

sunspot cooler, dark patch on the Sun

supernova huge explosion of a dying star

total eclipse of the Sun when the face of the Sun is completely covered by the Moon

universe everything in space, including Earth and millions of stars and planets

Find out more

Books

First Space Encyclopedia, Caroline Bingham (DK, 2008)

Comets (*Trailblazers*), David Orme (Ransom, 2006)

Stars and Galaxies (*Astronaut Travel Guides*), Isabel Thomas (Raintree, 2013)

Websites

hubblesite.org/gallery
On this website you'll find amazing photos from all over the universe, taken via the Hubble Space Telescope.

solarsystem.nasa.gov/kids/comets_kids.cfm
This website from NASA provides information about comets.

www.exploratorium.edu/eclipse/index.html
The Exploratorium is a great website for finding out about science and space. It includes instructions on how to make your own pinhole camera.

www.kidsastronomy.com
This website has everything you need to know about space. Click on "The Sky Tonight" to find out about star constellations you can see today.

www.sciencekids.co.nz/videos/earth/northernlights.html
Visit this website to watch a video of the Northern Lights.

Index